Contents

Just Another One is a collection of 25 poems that reflect the quiet, internal landscape of a deeply observant soul navigating the complexities of modern life. These poems are not grand proclamations or decorative verses—they are raw, thoughtful, and often uncomfortable reflections of what it means to be human in a world that often demands performance over presence.

The series explores themes such as emotional restraint, existential confusion, social constructs, love, detachment, fear, and the paradox of individuality in a collective world. Each poem stands alone in its voice and subject, but together they form a layered narrative—a journey inward, through stillness, silence, rebellion, observation, and finally, understanding.

The recurring phrase "just another one" becomes a quiet refrain throughout the collection, grounding the reader in the reality that we are all unique, yet fundamentally the same. It's a phrase that shifts in tone—sometimes it speaks of invisibility, other times of quiet strength, defiance, or surrender.

This series does not aim to offer solutions or tidy conclusions. Instead, it invites reflection. It opens a space where contradiction can exist without being resolved. Where one can be both deeply feeling and emotionally detached. Where belief and doubt sit side by side.

At its core, Just Another One is not about finding answers.

It is about acknowledging the complexity of asking honest questions—and letting them echo in stillness.

Prologue: The Quiet Voice in the Crowd

There are billions of us—
walking, talking, building, believing.
And in the noise of all that being,
the quiet ones often go unheard.

This is not a book of answers.
It is a series of moments—
soft awakenings, hard truths,
honest doubts, and fragile hopes.

It is not a rebellion,
but neither is it surrender.

These 25 poems belong to the one
who doesn't shout to be seen,
who watches more than he speaks,
who feels more than he reveals.

He is just another one—
and maybe,
so are you.

The One Who Watches

Just another mute spectator
to the slow-motion film of my life—
where scenes blur,
but silence is loud.

I drift like a paper boat
on a restless river—
no oars, no compass,
only stars to guide me.

Why should I chase the winds
that race past me,
or mourn the waves
that pull others ahead?

I walk barefoot on time's warm sand,
each footprint mine alone.
Some run,
some crawl—
but we all reach the one place
where the river stills,
where the sky folds us
into the same soft night.

There, we shall all rest—
the quick,
the weary,
the ones who danced,
and the ones who simply watched.

THE ONE THAT STAYS

Who walks without burdens?
We all carry storms—
the emotional wreckage,
the silent screams,
the chaos curled inside.

But I choose stillness.
I sit behind the curtain
like a mute spectator,
watching the fire and the flood
rise, fall, and pass me by.

The aches come—
sharp as shattered glass.
The pain drifts—
like smoke without a flame.
Life, a ship with broken sails,
cruises on without a map.

And here I stand—
at the crossroads of then and now,
watching each sorrow take its turn,
each joy, brief and trembling,
bow out.

Over time, they fade—
melting into yesterday,
only to be replaced
by the one who knocks next.
Just another one.

THE ONE WITH REGRETS

We all carry regrets—
ghosts of steps we never took,
what-ifs that whisper in the dark,
curling around our ribs
like smoke from a dying flame.

What's been spoken echoes still,
what's been done
leaves its shadow behind.
Worry not—
you're not alone on this path.

In this long bandwagon of regrets,
you're not the only one.
You're just another one
riding quietly beside the rest.

Some wear masks of laughter,
some bury it deep,
but your eyes—
they flinch when truth walks in.
Your words—
they carry the weight of silence.

The One Who Stands Apart

Different or difficult—
what's the difference
when your soul doesn't fit the
mold?

They say you're hard to be with,
too much, too quiet, too intense—
difficult to understand.
But tell me,
who isn't different,
beneath the layers they've peeled
away?

Most just learned to bend—
to smile when they wanted to
scream,
to nod when their heart said no.
They wore their masks well.

Did you?

Did you fold yourself small
just to fit in?
Or did you stand
—barefoot, bruised—
with your truth in hand?

The one who makes your life
difficult—
look closer.
It's not the world.
It's you,
the different one
who dares to accept his cracks,
who sees the fault lines
and doesn't look away.

The One Who Remembers Light

Most memories fade—
like rain on dry sand.
But some—
those rare, delicate few—
settle deep inside
and shape the way we breathe.

Many choose to cling
to the weight of sorrow,
drowning themselves
in oceans of what went wrong.

But I...
I am just a different one.

I gather the sparks—
the twinkle in your eyes
as if the stars blinked only for me,
the way your fingers brushed my palm—
gentle, unsure,
like a whisper with no words.

I remember the smile
that lit up my own—
not loud, not grand,
but enough
to warm even the coldest corner
of memory.

There have been moments of joy.
And I choose to hold them close—
not like anchors,
but like lanterns
guiding me through the dark.

The One Who Loved Forever

Like all idealists,
I longed for a forever kind of love—
one that stayed
long after the music faded.

Forever stayed with me.
Love didn't.
It evaporated—
like perfume on worn letters.

I am just another one,
love-lorn,
but not broken.
The only difference?

I remember—
the way laughter danced in the corners of your eyes,
how silence felt like a soft place to land,
how passion came without warning,
like summer rain on sun-baked skin.

Who has time to brood?
Who has time to drown in what left?
I chose to carry the feeling of forever—
not the one who walked away.

Because forever isn't a person.
It's a feeling that refused to leave.

THE ONE IN A HURRY

The ball slipped from my hand—
now it races down the hill,
gathering speed,
bouncing wild,
unbothered by what lies ahead.

My fate isn't mine anymore.
It rolls,
like that reckless ball,
dragging me
wherever the slope bends next.

I am not steering.
I am spinning,
blurring past faces and days,
hoping the ground stays kind.

Will the ball stop?
Yes—one day.
Even fate has a finish line.
And beyond that?
Stillness.
Silence.
The one full stop: death.

But until then,
let it roll.
Let the world blaze by—
a streak of light, a burst of sound.

Because I'm just another one
caught in motion,
in a hurry to live,
before it all comes
to rest.

The One Who Watches Her Leave

I see her walking away—
not in haste,
but with the quiet certainty
of someone who has already left inside.

I want to call,
shout,
scream—
but the noise of silence
is louder than all my longing.

She walks on,
and I cannot will her to stop.
Ego stands taller
than the trembling need in my chest.

If she must return,
she will.
But it must be her choosing—
not mine.
She picked her path,
and maybe,
just maybe,
her road will circle back to me.

I am just another hopeful—
a pitiful silhouette
framed against the sunset,
still waiting,
still watching,
as she dissolves into the horizon.

The One Suspended

The airplane hangs in the sky,
as if stitched into the clouds—
still,
and yet flying.

That's how I feel.
Suspended
in space and time,
while everything around me
spins,
spirals,
moves on.

I stand still,
or so it seems.
But maybe
I'm the one in motion—
and the world
is just standing still,
watching me flail in silence.

Who really moves?
Me,
or the rhythm I refuse to follow?
Does the world ever pause
and feel this too?

We hoard our feelings—
shut doors on empathy,
spend nothing but time.
We are thoughtless,
greedy
with our emotions.

I know I'm not the only one.
Just another drifting speck
in a sky that never lands.

The One Who Sees Through

In a world built on lies,
I'm just another one
searching for the grandest of them all—
the lie that dared to outlive truth,
that slipped past reason
and wore a crown of light.

The ultimate lie?
Religion.

It won.
It rose above laws of flesh and gravity,
broke nature's silence,
and whispered fear
into every soul that dared to dream freely.

It stole joy from the living,
wrapped it in shame,
and sold it back
as penance.

We became beggars—
apologizing for our breath,
pleading for what already exists—
sunlight, love, forgiveness,
all stamped "divine property"
before we could claim them as ours.

I am just another one—
not angry,
but awake.
And I will not pray
for what I already hold.

The One Who Forgot to Feel

Just another tear—
or many,
falling without sound,
without permission.

I sat in my chair,
still as stone,
watching them fall.
Numb.
My mind—a cyclone.
My face—a still lake.

Outside, I am calm.
Inside, I am chaos.

Like a rock,
I hold more than I show.
Hard on the outside,
plain,
unreadable.
But deep within—
a jewel forms,
pressed by years of silence.

The things that move me
swing wildly—
from love to loss,
from fury to joy.
But what I offer the world
is... blandness.
Blankness.
A quiet that says nothing.

I've forgotten
how to express.

Or maybe I just buried it—
with everything else
I didn't know how to hold.

The One Who Lets Go

Let them fly—
the emotions, the ache,
the tangled feelings.
Let them rise
and dissolve
into the ocean of nothingness.

Only then
do you begin to float—
free from the weight
you didn't know you carried.

I think this is why I write.
Not for meaning.
Not for beauty.
But for freedom.

Freedom from the slavery
of unspoken grief,
unfelt love,
unlived moments.

When it all pours out—
ink, breath, silence—
it becomes
scribbles on paper,
yes,
but also a map
to my own release.

And in the vastness left behind,
emptiness fills me.

I am just another seeker—
not of answers,
but of that clean, vast space
where nothing hurts
and everything simply is.

The kind of emptiness
that is full
of na
tural bliss.

The One Who Rises

The strength you seek
lives within.
People, moments, voices—
they offer support,
a hand,
a shoulder,
a little light.

But they cannot be your strength.
That fire must burn
in your own bones.

And when it does,
you'll draw more from the world,
not to survive,
but to rise.

Like vapor—
invisible,
gathering quietly,
until it becomes cloud,
until it owns the sky.

Then it returns—
not soft,
but strong—
a torrent that feeds rivers,
moves mountains,
carves its name into the land.

That's the kind of strength
I seek.
And when I find it,
I won't just survive—
I'll rule sky and earth
as one whole storm.

The One Who's Not Performing

The sincerity should shine through.
But who really cares—
in a world where filters speak
louder than truth?

Where the glitter of Reels,
the curated chaos of Shorts,
paint a life of
perpetual happiness,
on loop.

Smile. Post. Repeat.
Even grief must be beautiful now.

Virtual joy
pushing reality
off the edge—
where the algorithm doesn't reach,
but the loneliness does.

Is this the truth?
Or is it just
a prettier version of a lie
we all agreed to like?

Take it as entertainment—
that's all it is.
Scroll, don't feel.
Laugh, don't think.

As for me—
I'd rather fade from the feed.
I'd rather be
the forgotten one
who still remembers
how to feel
without an audience.

The One Who Took the Blame

Being at the top
is a thankless place.
But I am just another one—
and I have no regrets.

Climb as high as you like,
and still,
no one thanks you.
But stumble once,
and a thousand fingers rise,
sharp as spears.

They'll say you offended them,
wounded their pride,
when all you did
was speak what they refused to hear.

This world—
built on polished lies,
prefers applause to truth.

Praises?
We wear them like medals.
But criticism?
We toss it like poison
and search for someone else to blame.

I've seen it.
I've lived it.
And I say—
have the courage
to hold both sides of the coin.
Not just the shine.
Hold the weight,
the dirt,
the truth.

The One Who Let Go in Time

We hold on to things—
memories, grudges, fears—
until the shelves of our soul
groan under the weight.

We hoard them like secrets,
until every empty space
is no longer empty.

The cupboard creaks
when you try to close it.
So does the heart.

We bottle it all—
anger, grief, unspoken words—
tightly,
like it's noble
to stay silent.

But when the dam breaks,
when that one small crack
lets everything through—
it's too late.

Floodwaters don't ask permission.
They drown what's in their path—
friendships, trust, love.

We regret,
but by then,
so much has already
gone under.

I am just another one
learning this late—
that strength
is not in holding on.
It's in the small release,
the whispered confession,
the timely tear.

Be the one
who doesn't wait
for the flood.
Let it flow.
Let it breathe.
Let it go.

The One Without Colors

There's a fine line
between two Ps—
personal
and professional.

We pretend they don't blur,
but they do—
quietly,
like ink bleeding through paper.

Only a few
know how to keep them apart.
They are the ones who endure.
Who don't crumble.
Who last.

Like a tree—
dependent on sun, rain, soil,
and yet
standing alone,
tall,
untouched by the noise around it.

He is that tree.
The one who does not
live in shades of gray.

Black or white.
Yes or no.
All or nothing.

No space for color,
no room for maybes.

I am just another one
who's learning
to stop needing the rainbow,
and start living in contrast.

The One Who Stopped Chasing Freedom

We all clamor for freedom—
shout it, chase it,
bleed for it.

But are we ever truly free?
Or is freedom
just another illusion
shaped by perception?

I, for one,
no longer seek it.

I know
I will always be bound—
by gravity,
by breath,
by the quiet laws of nature
that hold everything in place.

I am a slave
to hunger and longing,
to dreams that wake me
and fears that lull me to sleep.

Desires, needs,
flickers of want—
they pull the strings.
They write my days.

Why should I chase
what was never mine?
Why dream of something
that cannot exist
within this flesh,
within this cycle?

I am just another one,
accepting my place
in the circle of life and death—
and everything quiet
in between.

The One Who Dared to Try

Don't shy away
from something new.

Who knows—
it might show you a future
you never even dreamed of.

A path you never walk
can never reveal
its hidden turns,
its secret destinations.

Take the leap.

If you keep doing
what you've always done,
in the same way,
again and again—
don't be surprised
when the results don't change.

You want a new life?
Then live it differently.

Try something unfamiliar.
Say yes
when fear says no.
Turn left
where you've always gone right.

I am just another one
who learned
that the door doesn't open
until you knock on the one
you never noticed before.

Who knows—
your next step
might bring you closer
to the life
that's been waiting all along.

The One Who Saw Himself in Others

When you finally find
yourself
within yourself—
not the mask,
not the noise,
but the true shape of you—

you begin to find
pieces of that self
in every person you meet.

Only when you sit with your silence
can you hear the silence in others.
Only when you feel your ache
can you recognize theirs.

Maybe they're lonely, too.
Maybe they're just waiting
for someone to stay.
To ask.
To listen.
To see them.

We move fast—
hearing without listening,
looking without seeing,
passing each other
like shadows in motion.

I am just another one—
one of the crowd,
wondering
how many of us
are quietly
hoping
to be understood.

The One Who Didn't Run

We're called social beings—
wired for connection,
built for belonging.

But our actions
betray the title.
We push, grab, race—
without looking back,
without knowing
what we're racing toward.

No finish line.
No purpose.
Just motion.

We get tired.
We long to rest.
But the moment we pause,
we see them—
everyone else still running.

And so we run, too.

But then,
there is just this one—
he stops.
He watches.
The world spins past him
like a carousel of noise and light.
He says nothing.
He just lets it all pass.

And there's this other one—
the louder one.
He also stops,
but he shouts, points, waves,
demands to be seen.

And us,
the intelligent ones—
we follow him.
Not the quiet one.
Never the quiet one.

THE ONE WHO ENVIED THE ANTS

The ants
are better than us.

At least they know
where they're going
and why.

There's no competition—
just a line,
one after another,
moving with purpose.

They find food.
They return with it.
They serve a reason
larger than themselves.

If a wall appears,
they don't complain.
They climb over it.
Go around it.
Adapt.

They are not loud.
They are not lost.
They just are.

But we—
we chase,
we build,
we hoard,
we sprint.

And ask ourselves,
mid-race,
what the race was for.

We are just those ones—
moving with urgency,
driven by noise,
purposeful in stride
but
without any real purpose.

The One Who Questioned Fear

We have emotions—
soft, unguarded, real.
And we are affected
by everything around us—
the noise,
the silence,
the stories we're fed.

From the moment we are conceived,
we are conditioned—
to fear.

Not danger,
but the idea of danger.
The fear of fear itself.
The monsters that aren't there.

The biggest of them all—
God.

Heaven and hell—
some fiction
written by some
to rule the many.

The diktats of the unseen,
the faceless,
the nameless,
passed down like law,
like chains made of belief.

We obey,
we pray,
we kneel
to the ghosts of power.

I am just another one—
living quietly
under their invisible thumbs,
wondering
if freedom begins
the moment we stop
being afraid.

The One Among the Many

We are social animals—
we need a society,
we build one,
cling to it,
survive through it.

But why?

Were we not born alone—
wailing, screaming,
entering a world
without knowing a soul?

Will we not die alone—
in silence,
in stillness,
no matter who stands beside us?

And yet,
between birth and death,
we reach for others.

Family. Friends.
Familiar hands
to hold our fears,
echo our laughter,
witness our lives.

And still—
we betray, we wound, we destroy
our own.

A strange species—
needing connection,
and yet so good at tearing it apart.

I am just another one—
a cog in this great, rusted wheel
of longing and forgetting.
Turning because I must.
Not always knowing why.

The One Who Looked Up

In the timeline of the universe,
our voyage
is infinitesimally small—
a blink, a breath,
a whisper in the dark.

Yet we walk as though
we own it.
As though stars were born
to light our path.

The higher one goes,
the smaller we appear—
until, finally,
we vanish.
Invisible. Insignificant.

And still—
we try to master the cosmos,
bend it, tame it,
enslave what cannot be owned.

But the universe has no master.
It doesn't need one.

We are just a spark—
a flicker of dust
blessed with thought,
burdened by ego.

So intelligent,
we call destruction
a kind of construction.

We tear apart
to build
what won't last.

I am just another one—
small, aware,
floating in the endlessness,
finally still enough
to wonder
what it means
to be part of something
I'll never understand.

EPILOGUE: THE ECHO THAT REMAINS

What began as a whisper
became a map.
Not of cities,
or stars,
but of feelings—
those quiet forces
we're taught to hide.

These poems were never meant to fix
anything.
They simply **stood beside the truth**,
like a friend who doesn't interrupt your
silence.

And now, at the end,
there is no grand awakening,
no promised redemption.
Only stillness.
Only space.
And the knowing
that being "just another one"
might be the most honest thing we ever
are.

If this voice felt like yours,
it's because it was.

Manish Prasad is a quiet observer in a noisy world.
A teacher by profession and a wanderer by nature,
his writing is rooted in deep reflection, emotional
clarity, and an unwavering honesty. He writes not to
impress—but to express. Through his poetry, Manish
gently challenges illusions, invites silence, and
reminds us that we are all, in some way, just
another one—searching, feeling, breaking, healing.
This is his second poetic offering, following the soul-
stirring journey of The Wanderer's Lust.
He writes with no pretensions—only presence.

Just Another One

Manish Prasad

www.ingramcontent.com/pod-product-compliance
Lightning Source LLC
Chambersburg PA
CBHW040858110726
48005CB00001B/111